This book was published by Hard Press, Inc., a non-profit organiztion, in association
with Pamela Auchincloss, Arts Management, under whose auspices a traveling exhibition
was organized to coincide with this publication.

We would like to thank the Butler Institute of American Art, Douglas Cramer,
John Macleod and Ann Klee, John Raimondi and Ralph Cantin, the Rubell Family Collection,
Mr. and Mrs. Burt Aaron, and Peter Stephan for generously agreeing to loan their paintings
to the traveling exhibition.

All works were photographed by Gunther Knop, with the
exception of "Flatford Mill" which was done by Americolor.

Designed by Jonathan Gams and Gary Stephan.

Printed In China

ISBN: 1-889097-30-6

Same Body
Different Day

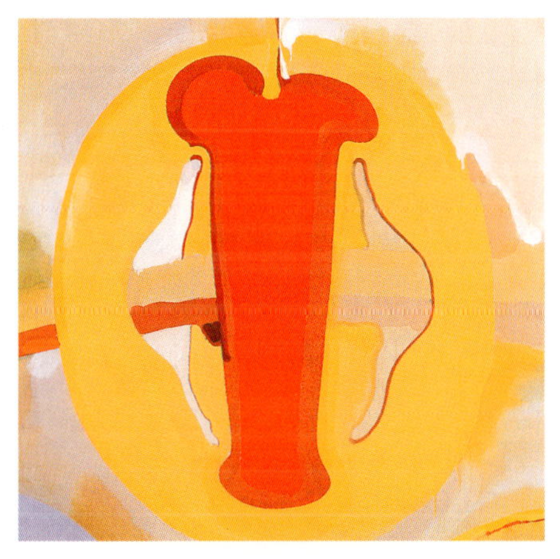

Gary Stephan

Text by Peter Schjeldahl

These last ten years have seen the opening up of my work by paradoxically bringing things together.

This book which so clearly reflects this is possible because Pamela Auchincloss
said it should be done and Alex Muse said it would be done.

To John Raimondi, Douglas Cramer, Peter Stephan, and Hank McNeil
whose generosity turned desires into facts.

To Jon Gams who encouraged me to design this book with him
and made the unfamiliar world of computers a true pleasure.

Peter Schjeldahl's text was at first frighteningly and ultimately happily close
to having someone feel around inside my heart.

Over the years I have felt that David Shirey cared about my fate and his generous
concern led to Lou Zona's enthusiastic acceptance of this project.

These acknowledgements are framed by the friendship of Gregory Amenoff
who introduced Pamela to me.

And to my brother Peter, my cohort in things visual.

And ultimately to my sensational wife Suzanne Joelson who never
let me loose sight of this book coming into being.

Concerning the Spiritual in Gary Stephan

What is spirituality, why is it a hot topic today, and how have contemporary painters become authoritative about it? Gary Stephan's recent work points to these questions. It's not because he has changed dramatically. He has changed somewhat, at his usual, gradual, self-freshening rate. Least of all has Stephan, a sturdy agnostic, somehow gotten religion. (The story I will tell here is all mine.) But lately the world has altered around him in ways that sharply dramatize a constant concern of his art. That concern involves our willingness to believe in abstract visual illusions.

A robust presence in New York painting for nearly three decades, Stephan has always been a dancing master of painterly devices cultivated for their own sake. He still is. His works remain propositions about elegance. He tacitly offers art's most reliable reason for asking us to credit visual fiction: pleasure. We will be happier playing along than not playing along. This would be enough, still, but now a larger appeal adds itself to the picture.

Stephan practices what Clement Greenberg called, apropos abstract paintings with suggestive elements, "homeless representation." Another epithet comes to mind, Marianne Moore's definition of poetry: "imaginary gardens with real toads in them." Stephan deploys catchy, evocative shapes in illusionistic space, where they often behave to the eye as if possessed of natural gravity or buoyancy. He sets perception and metaphor in quivering tension, subtly and delightfully. We savor their interactions as if they were characters in a play or film.

Unreal adventures of emblematic entities are a familiar trope of abstract painting, grounded in Kandinsky, Malevich, and Mondrian. It looks easy, and fundamentally it has become so. Credulous susceptibilities of our eyes and minds, which modern artists (plus cartoonists and advertisers) have explored exhaustively, make us suckers for learnable tricks with figure and ground, say. Meanwhile, homeless representation's easy charm renders it hard to direct with intelligence and poise—let alone, as when Stephan does it, with wit and loveliness.

In itself, the trope means nothing. It is just another of the means by which pictures affect us. It is a technical matter. But being affected—being induced to think and feel in particular ways—is not a technical but, loosely speaking, a spiritual matter. Our speaking about spirituality is looser at some times than at others. It is ever less casual today. Stephan's past mastery of pictorial ambiguity takes on new urgency to the extent that our attention to it is newly searching and anxious.

Spirituality names our attitude, the deepest of which the mind is capable, toward what we cannot know. It is not a content or category of thought. It is an event. It occurs at the mental perimeter where the light of consciousness, and even the dusky glow of the so-called unconscious, fades to the profound blackness of organic process—which in its turn, at some unfathomable verge in a manner impossible to conceive of, segues into the universe of everything that is dead.

Perhaps some people never contemplate this dire frontier, persisting instead on life's upsurge like ping-pong balls aloft on fountains, but I think that such people are rare. More commonly, spiritual experience in our society is a dark and inchoate, lonely phenomenon, kept mute by a kind of shame. Our own intellects may recoil from it with dread or with the indignation of injured pride. But there come moments in nearly every life when inner floodgates fly open and mystery inundates us. Are the moments good or bad, wonderful or terrible?

When they happen, we sense ourselves objectified—and diminished almost if not utterly to nothing—in the regard of an all-encompassing, all-dissolving reality. Our emotional state in that last ditch of ourselves constitutes our spiritual condition. Is it hysterical? Is it reverent? Do we feel that the great reality is benign or malignant, aware or absurd? Not only do these questions matter, no other question may truly matter except in relation to them.

Here is an understatement: a psychic consequence of the 20th century in the West is disappointment with reason. Humanity was to be redeemed by science and politics, psychoanalysis and revolution. Didn't happen. A long war of intellect against spirit ends in defeat—despite the fact that, in society, organized religions keep declining. Contrary to the fancies of modern thinkers, it was never modern thought that threatened religion but always modernity itself, whose shattering effects continue unabated. Though we no longer term our hurtling movement "progress," we move unstoppably, head over heels, into an arbitrary future.

Lacking cohesive religion, spirituality itself is homeless today, and the echo of its impasse in Stephan's art strains the limits of metaphor. Impasse and art register as a virtual identity. I hasten to say that this conjunction is incidental to the paintings' quality as paintings. Big meanings by themselves don't improve art, as small meanings don't diminish it. But, in how we value any object of our experience, there is a scale of significance besides a scale of goodness. On that scale, my own long-held admiration for Stephan soars.

An English medieval mystic observed that we mistakenly feel close to things that we have clear ideas of. The truth is opposite. Clarity measures our distance from an object of thought. Ultimate reality, wrote the anonymous mystic, is met with in a "cloud of unknowing." Compare some frequent remarks of the great American pragmatist William James, to the effect that we accord mental vagueness too little intellectual dignity. In such vagueness, the roots of our being clutch for nourishment.

Stephan is a precisionist of the vague, the half-thought, the intuitive, the incipient—things on the tip of the tongue, just around the corner, barely out of reach. We hate such indeterminate sensations, as a rule. Stephan's lyrical skill makes us begin to love them, as they must be loved if we are ever to be contented with our actual existence. In a way, nothing is more concrete to our minds than honest vagueness that does not resolve into forced certainty—though our yen for certainty is pretty concrete, too.

Stephan's new paintings play with the yen. They are full of resolved shapes—mostly ellipses and odd, totemic motifs—that declare their confidence with brazen colors like red and orange or, sullenly, in black. The generally paler painted ground outside the shapes' contours obligingly goes atmospheric to accommodate them, but only while we look at the shapes. To a more diffuse gaze, the ground flips from negative to positive optical space. It commandeers a formal argument to which, abruptly, the shapes become futile objections.

The shapes project will. The ground maintains knowledge. The ground has the stronger case going in and, after the shapes filibuster, prevails in the end. Painting and painted ground are essentially one, as Greenberg correctly taught while preaching, fanatically, an elimination by painters of anything incidental to that recognition. But what, except death, isn't incidental? Art is incidental to life, which is incidental to the universe. Stephan invokes classical, Greenbergian formalism to investigate how incidents of art and life transpire—never mind whether they ought to.

We live and breathe until we don't any more, and meanwhile our eyes dart about our environment, hungry for stimulus. The best abstract painting, like Stephan's, rests its legitimacy on a persuasive identification of living with looking. All paintings are consciousness surrogates—fitting over our brains like virtual-reality helmets, such that we experience, as our own, thoughts and feelings that originate elsewhere. Abstraction aims to intensify this transaction's uncanniness, bending consciousness back on itself to make thought the material of thought and feeling the object of feeling.

Pleasure is indispensable here, or else our encounter with abstract painting would be an ordeal. But there are values that supersede pleasure. Otherwise we would perish of pleasure-seeking, like drug addicts. I think that higher values enter Stephan's current work by way of dissonant effects new to him—slightly harsh, abrading departures from his normal harmoniousness. One endures these notes of discomfort at first because, on balance, pleasure still predominates, then later because the irritation itself acquires significance.

Grown-up religious experience begins with the conviction that there is something wrong with us. Religions name it—as sin, say, or karma—and show how it may be redeemed by our submission to a universal power that is held to be somehow aware and essentially benign. Struggling despair thereby turns to accepting hope. For this to work, belief is indispensable. But even an unbeliever—as William James proved in his *Varieties of Religious Experience*—can see that it works indeed.

Belief is beyond the inner means of many of us for reasons good or bad but, at any rate, obdurate. I tend to believe in belief, at least. I know from conversation with Stephan that he doesn't, particularly. His is a secular, urbane vision that bets on the life-sustaining capacity of delicately managed aesthetic sensation. I insist only that, in his faithfulness to his vision and even without meaning to, Stephan provides timely grist to the timeless mill of the soul.

—Peter Schjeldahl

Paintings
1988 — 1998

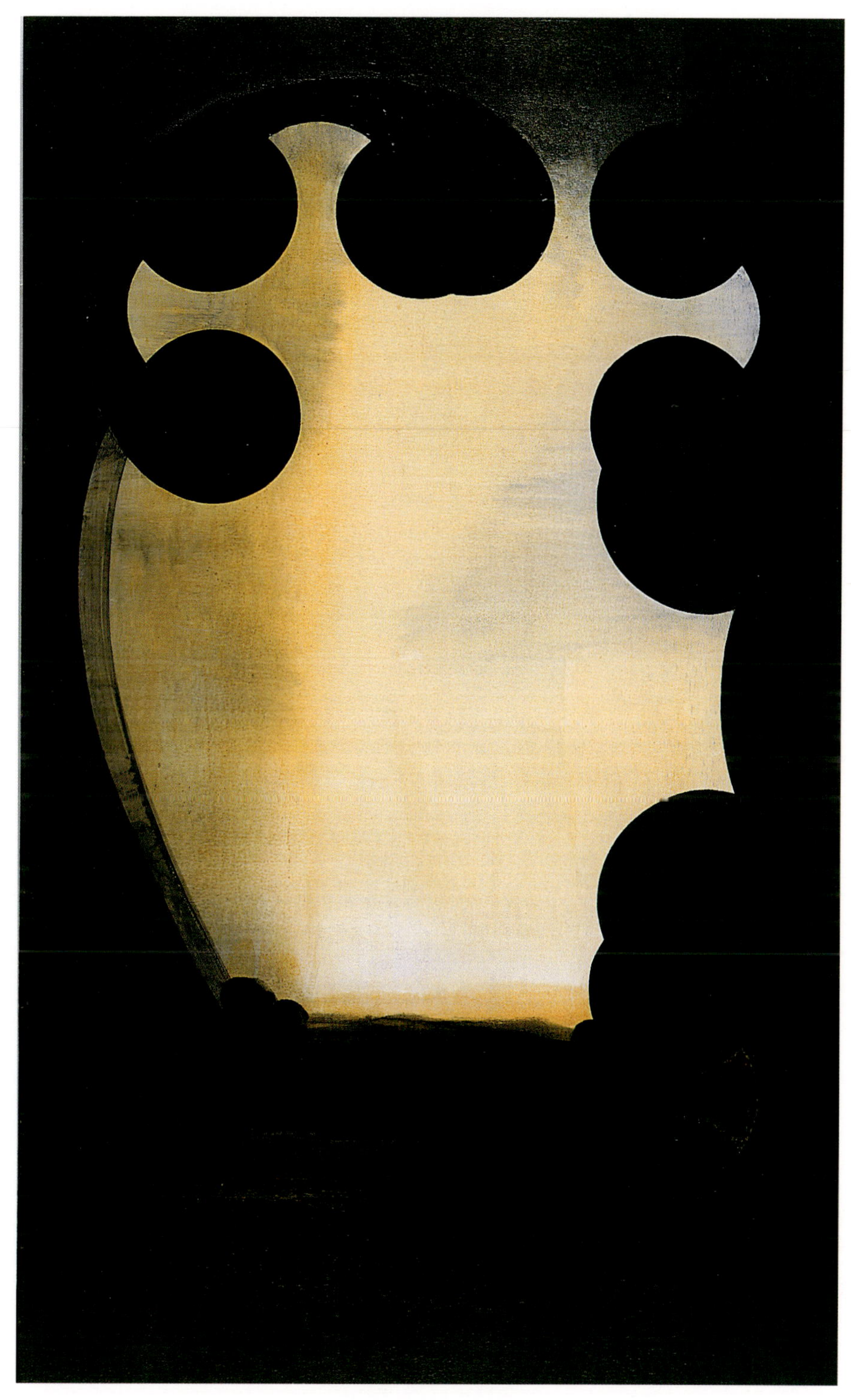

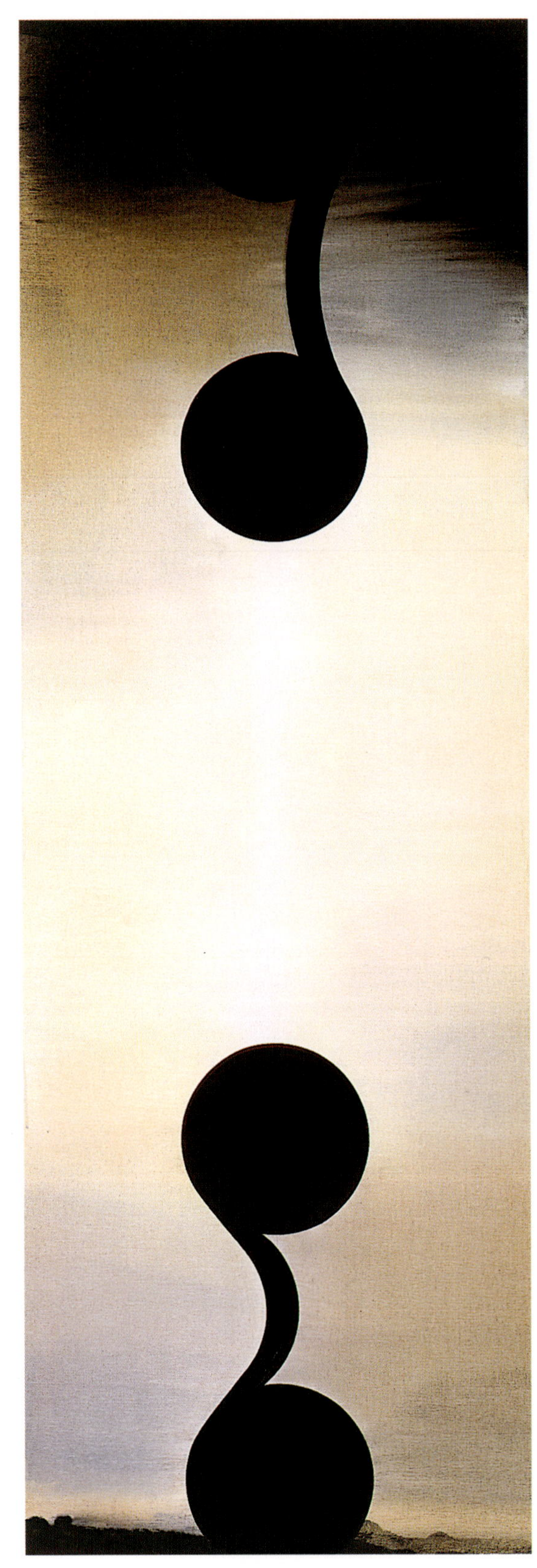

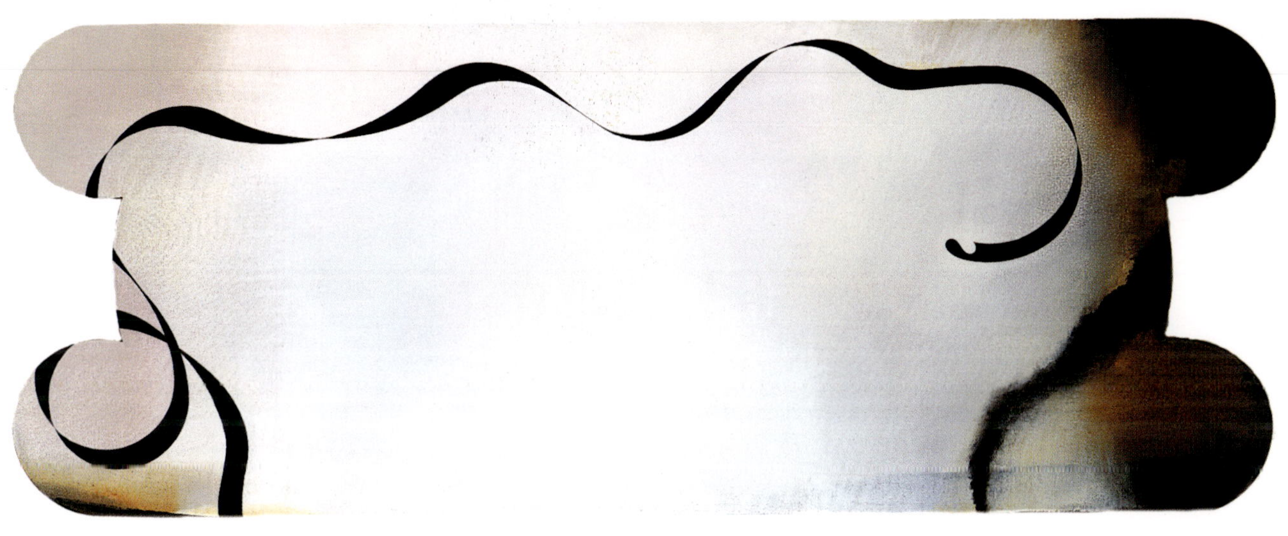

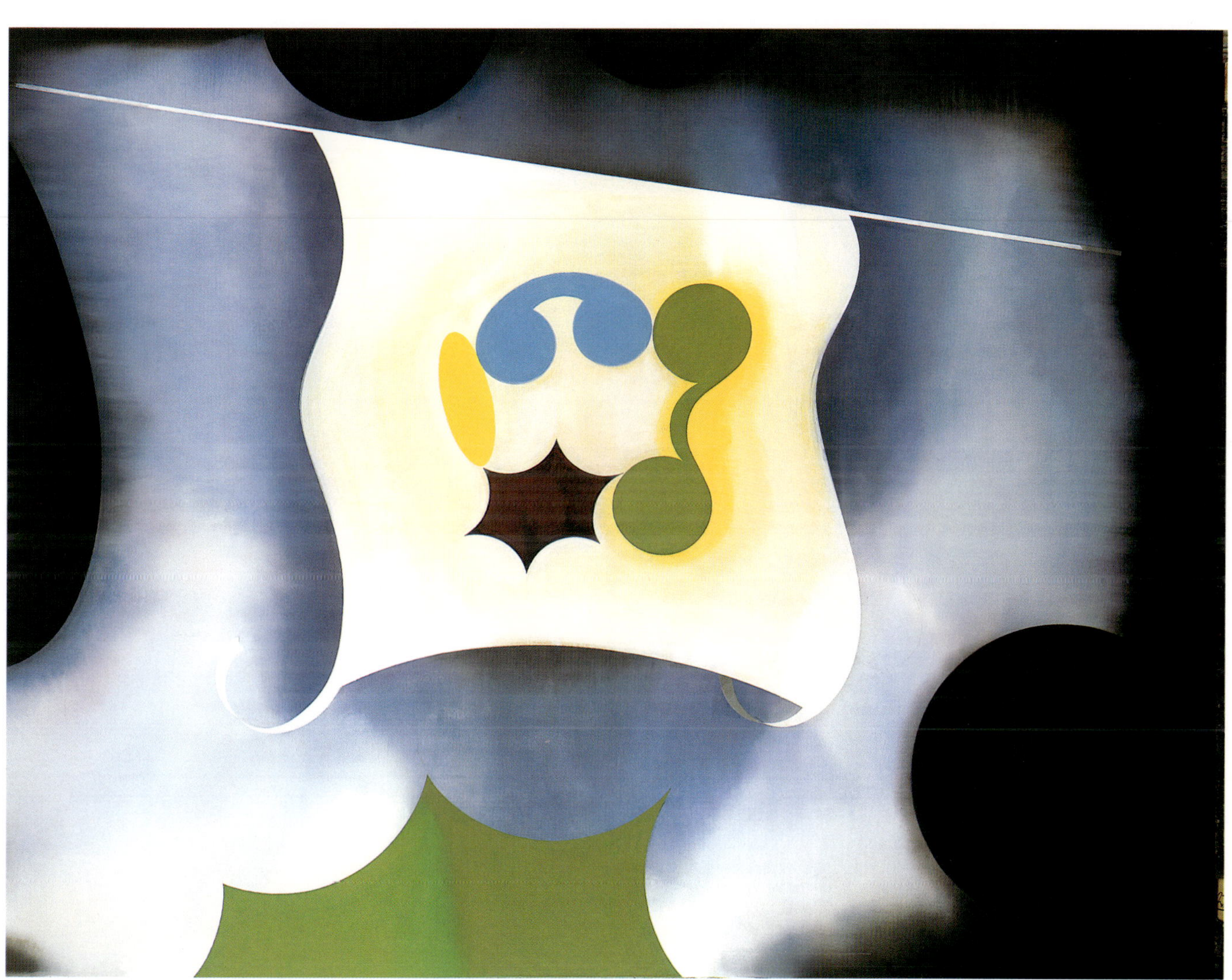

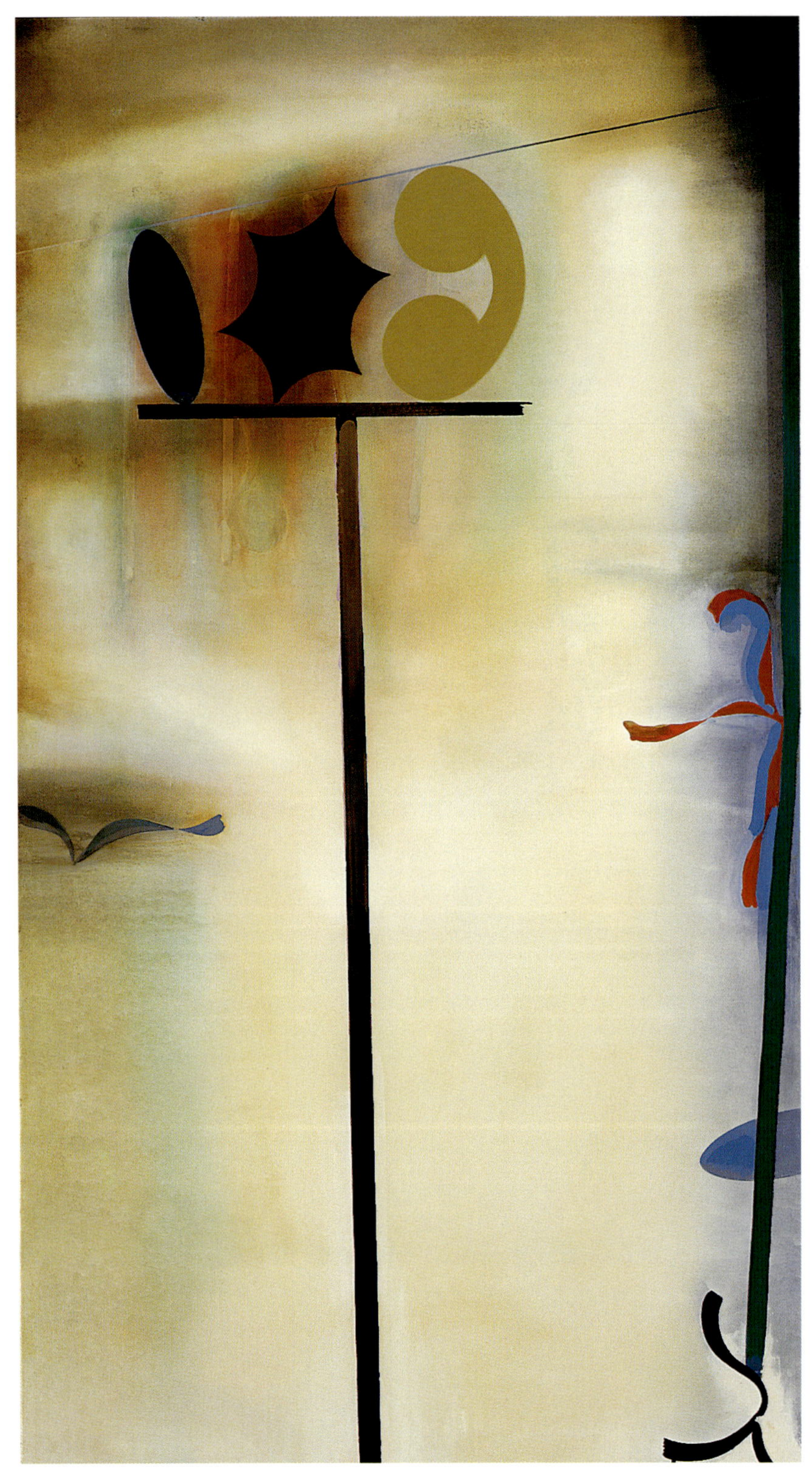

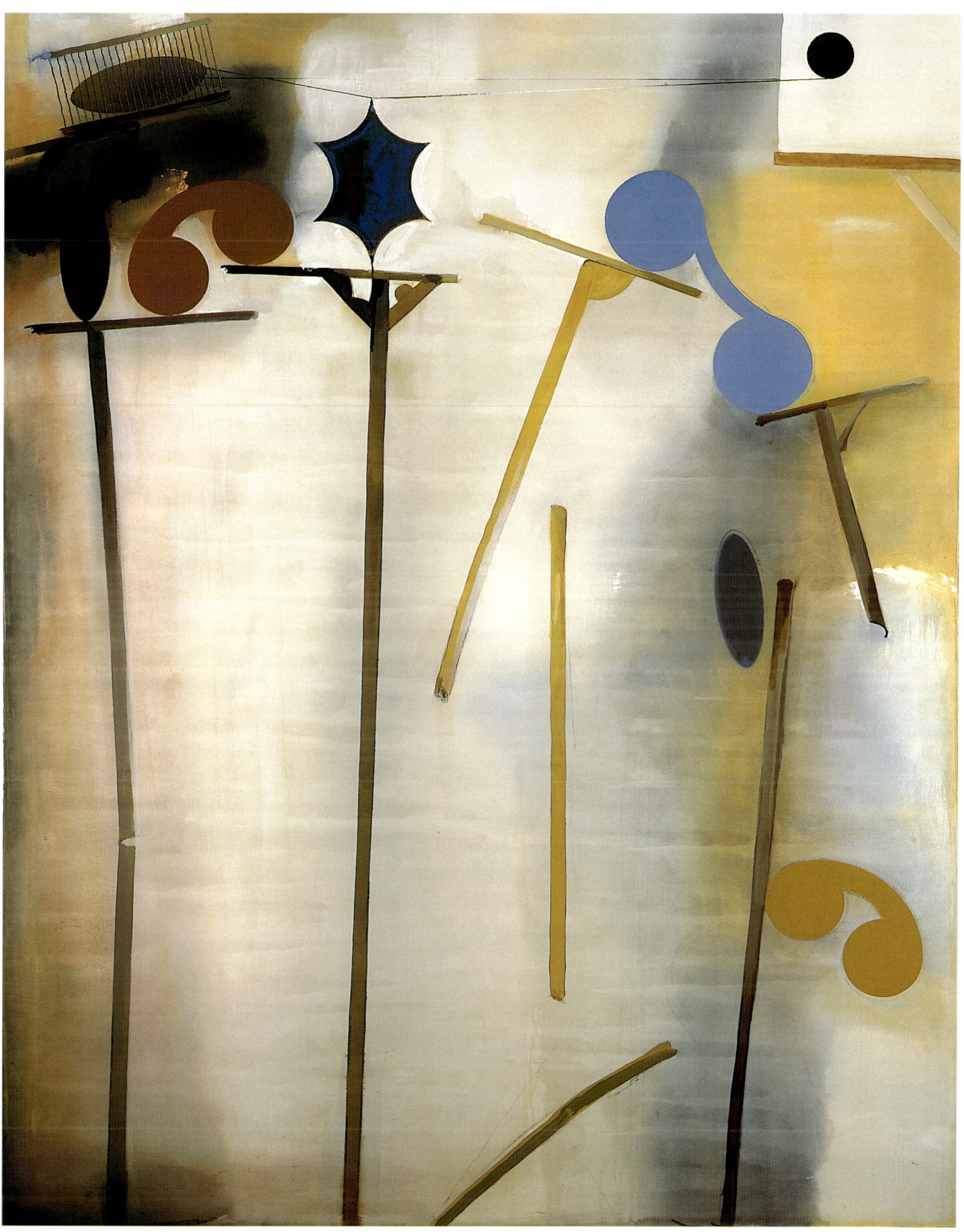

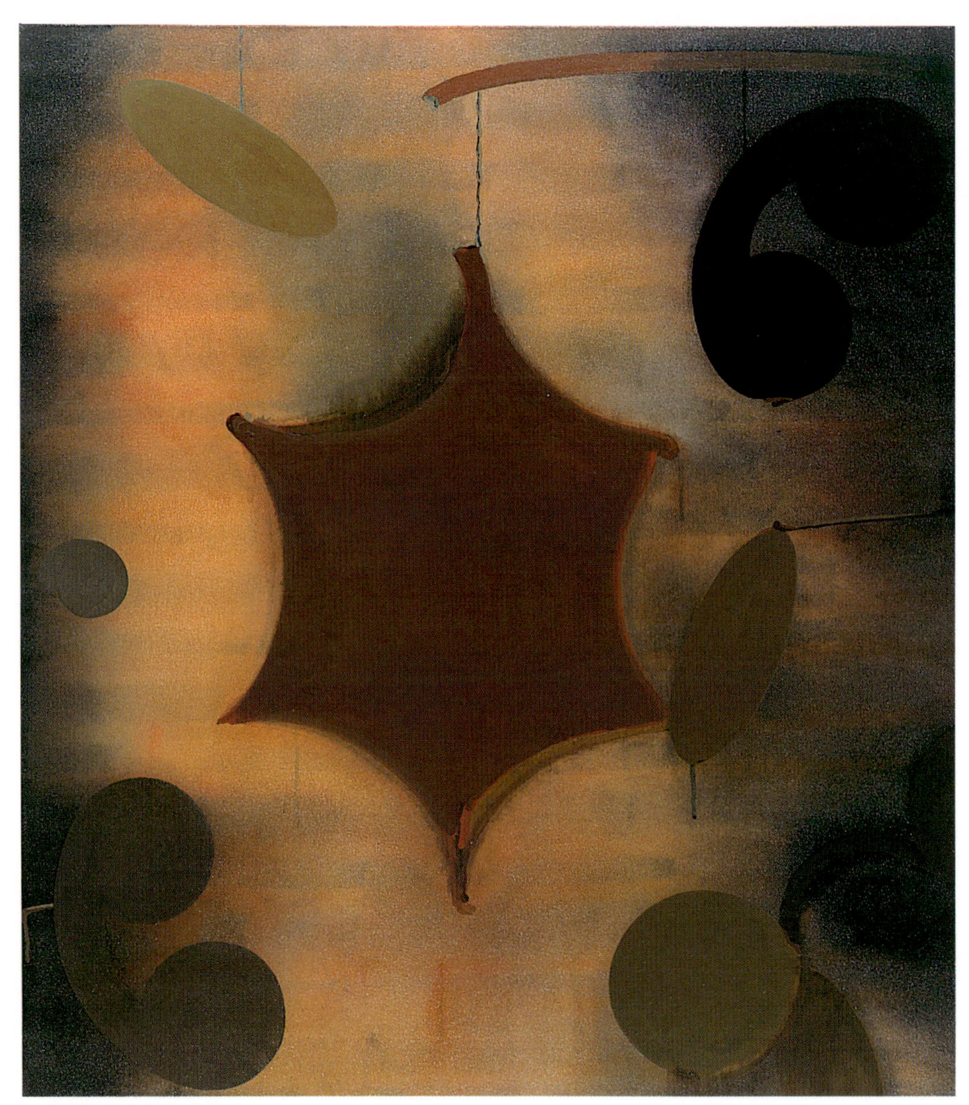

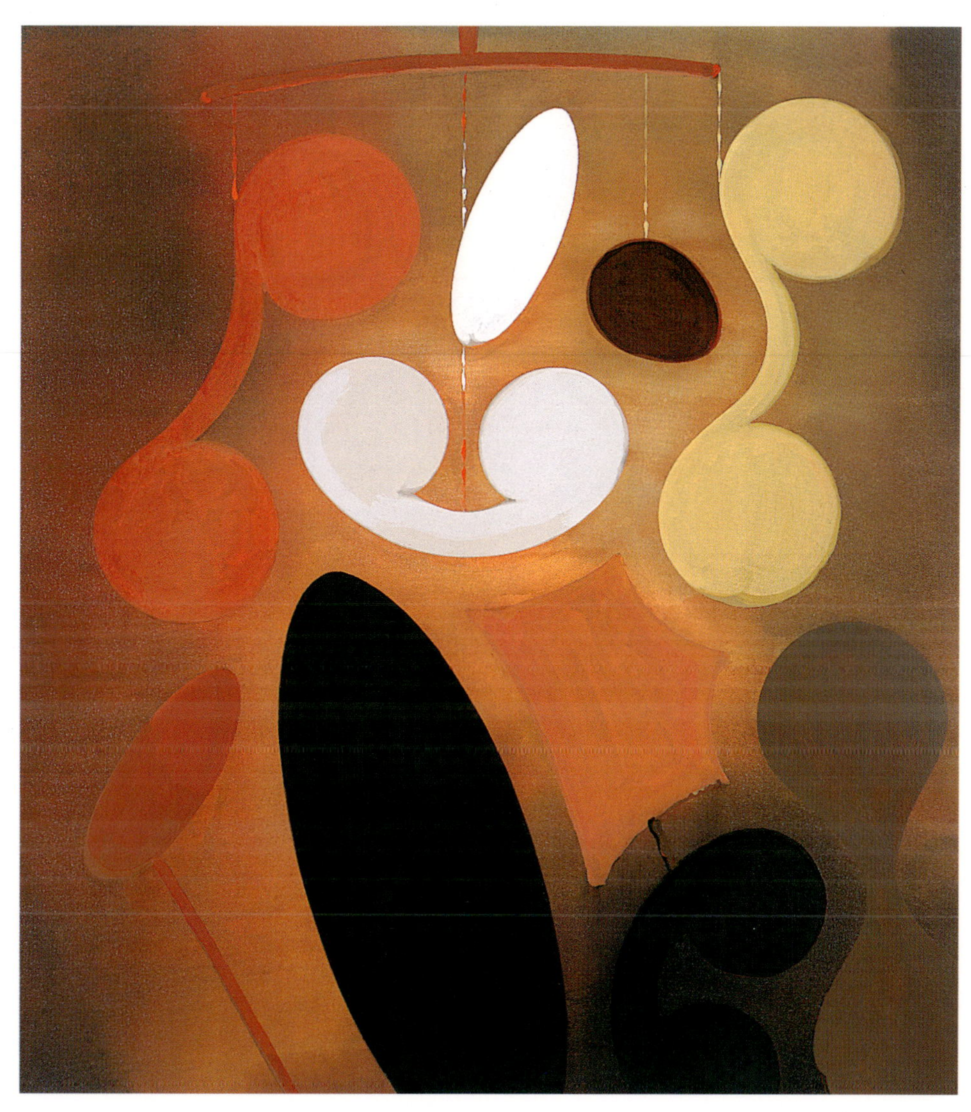

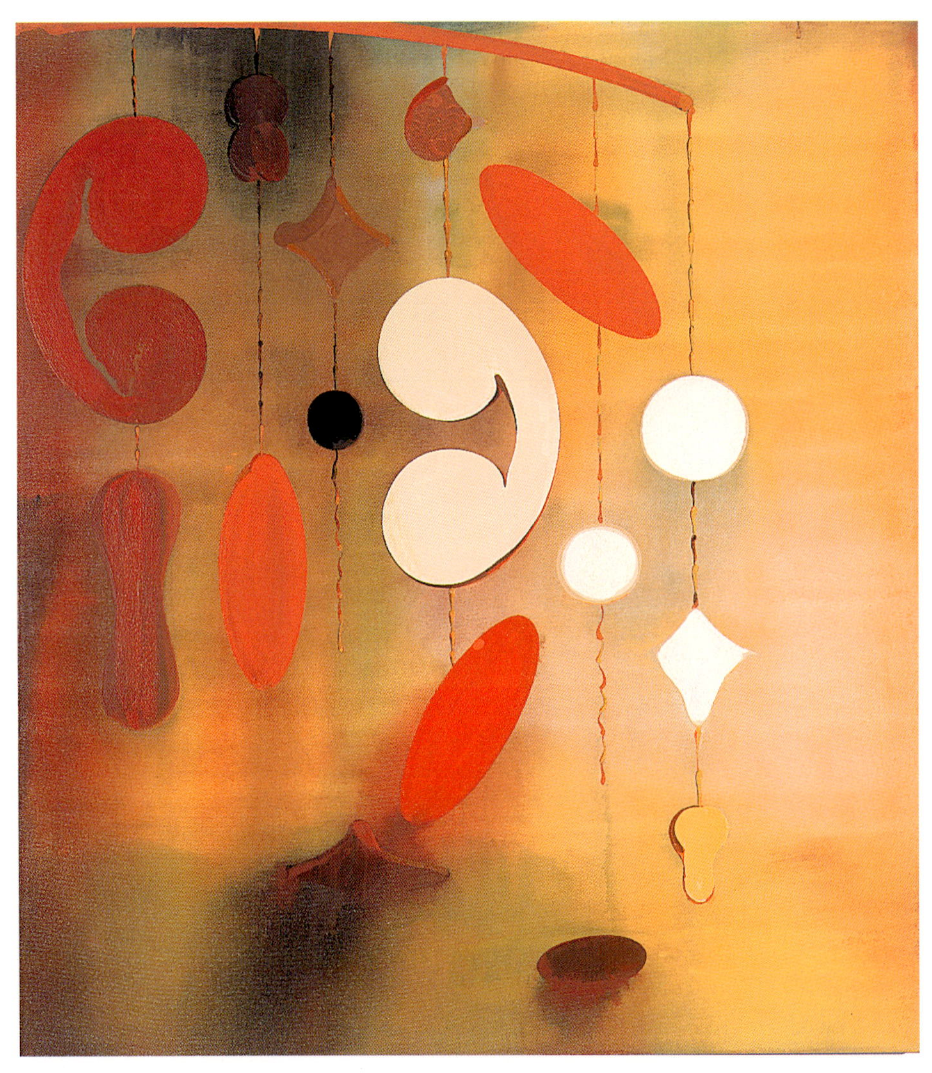

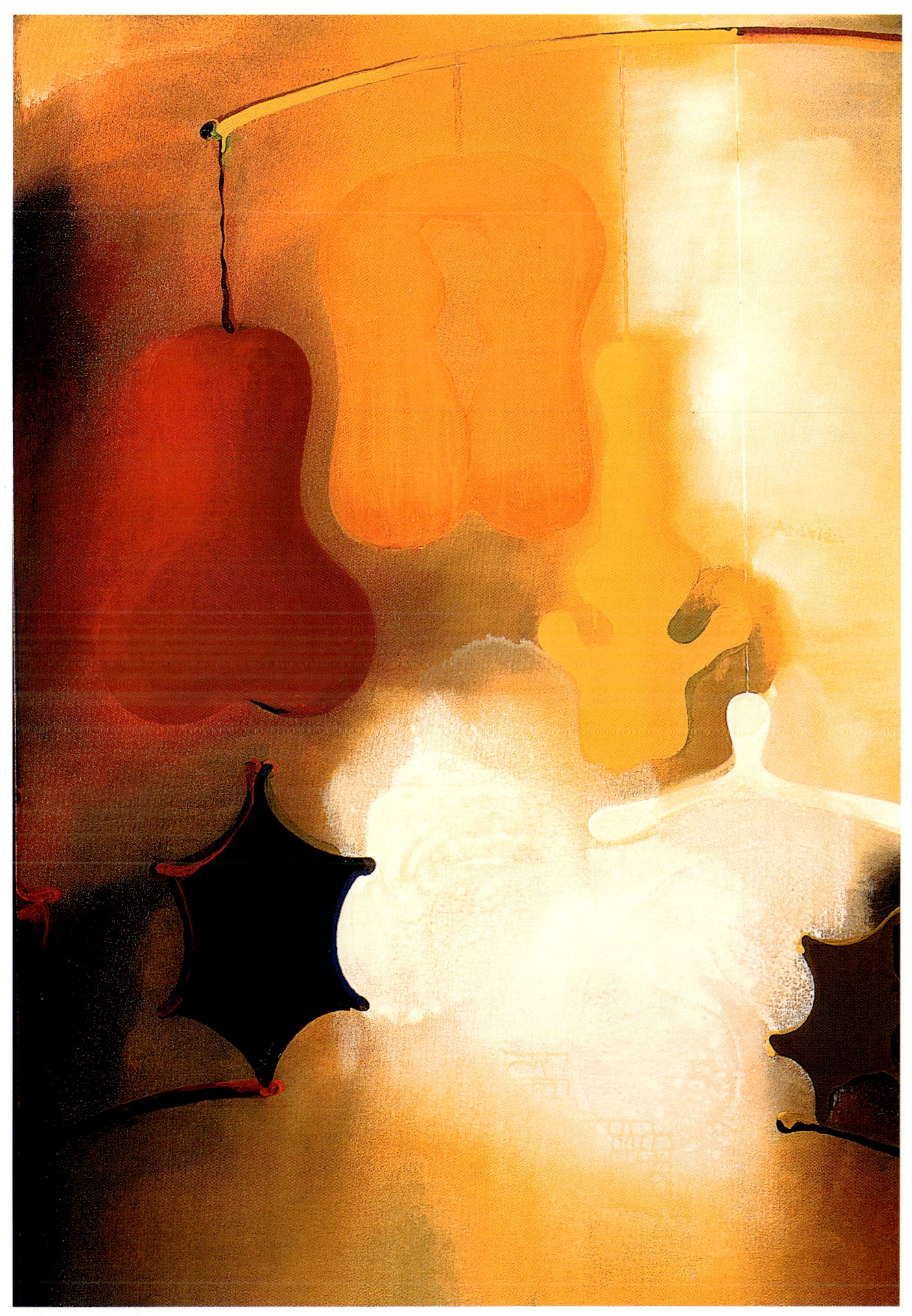

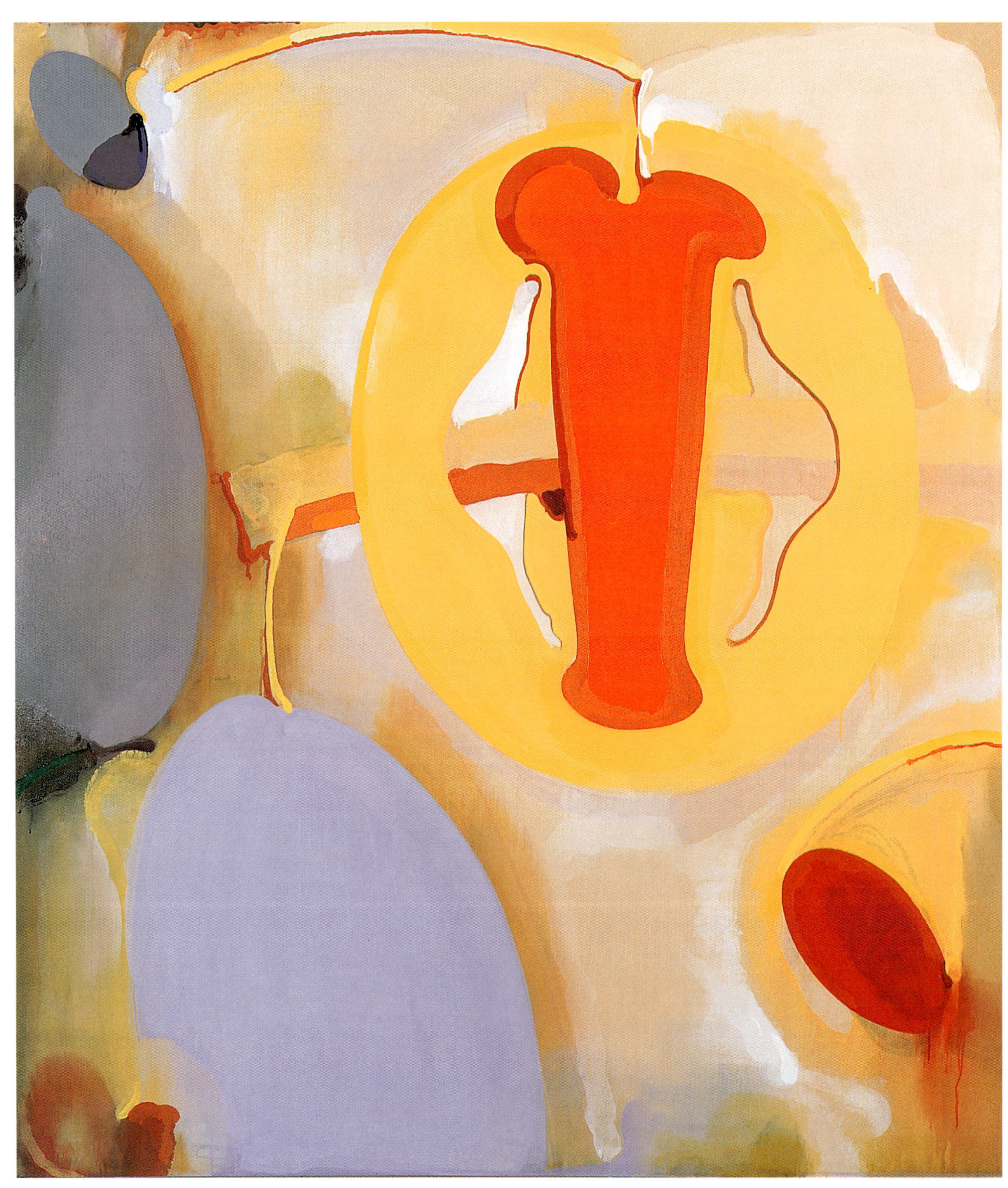

On the following pages are some found images from my studio. One is a photograph that the photographer Elliot Schwartz gave me of four gourds on a seed package onto which someone has placed four black dots which give the appearance of holes in the gourds. The addition of this kind of pure form drastically changes the meaning and possibilities of the gourd. Another is a photo of the coffee table from our living room which I took out to wash or something. It's in the shadow of the house, actually, and with the power of these two little lines—which are of course the legs—the abstract forms are rendered into a palpable space. This kind of "getting a lot for nothing" is the way my mind works on composition.

The relationship between the images on my wall and the content of the paintings is one of faith. I imagine that if you put things up that intrigue you and you don't avoid them but you don't solicit them, if you don't make yourself think about them but you don't ignore them—if they can get a neutral valence where they just sort of float— then, over time they'll make themselves appropriately evident. The degree to which they should be in a painting will show up naturally because they'll reflect my actual interest in them.

Things hang in these paintings or float or balance as a function of gravity. Before I introduced gravity into the pictures about 12 years ago there was no way to narrate the abstractions because they didn't do anything. You couldn't tell their destinies, you couldn't know their fates because they didn't work like anything in the real world. . . So, many of these hanging or suspended elements are the result of trying to see how you can make narrative-like structures in abstraction. Questions of memory in abstraction are moot because abstractions have no destiny, because we don't know how they were, so we can't know how they will be. A key point of modernism was to create this thing called presence which meant that the object as you found it was sufficient and that it wasn't to be attached to any other notion. In other words, it had no mortality and I thought if I'm going to allow abstraction to speak about mortality, or speak about the happenstances of a lived life, then I've got to re-narrate these things and gravity struck me as one of the fundamental ways.

—Gary Stephan, West Stockbridge, 1998

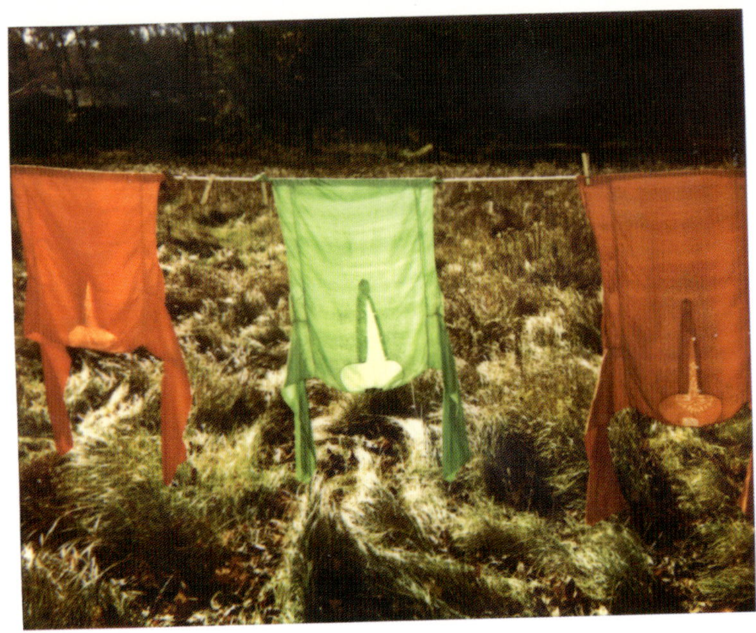

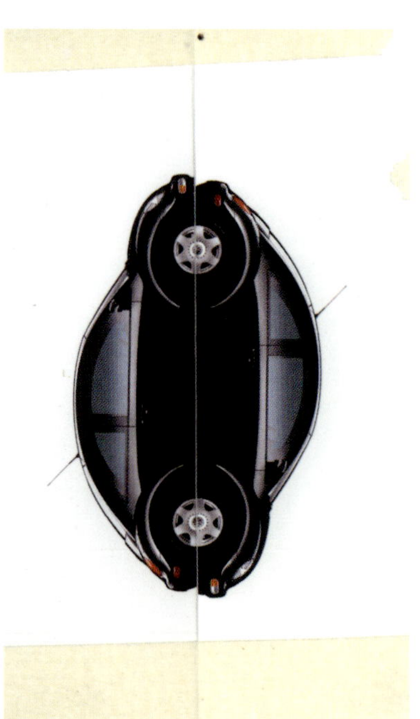

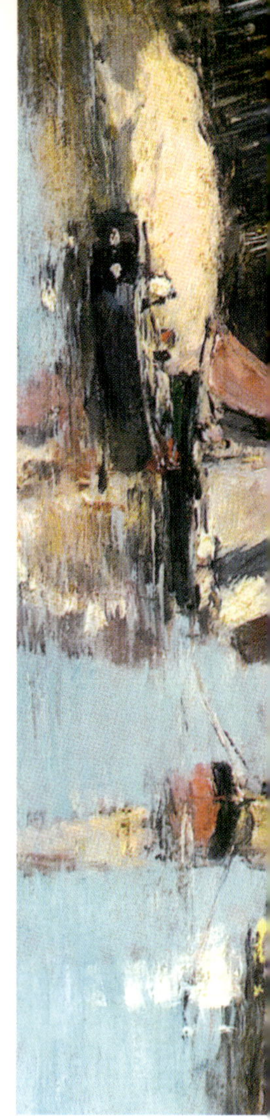

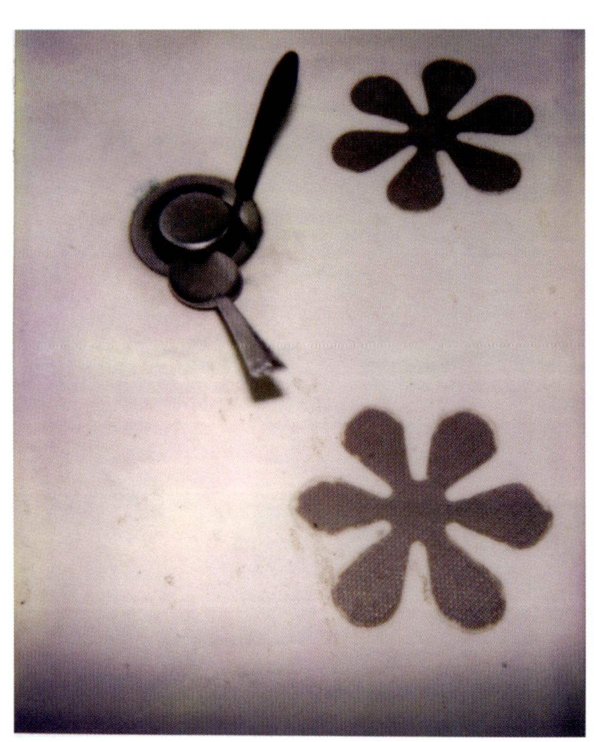

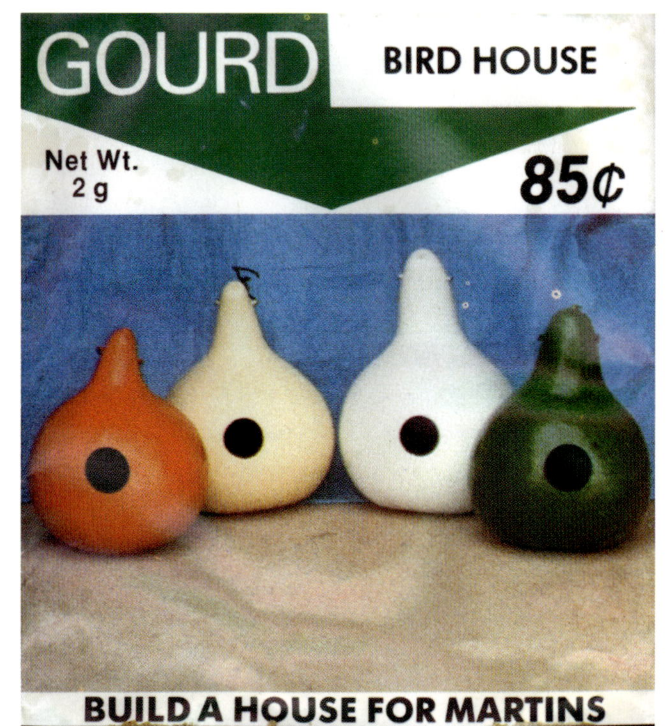
GOURD BIRD HOUSE
Net Wt.
2 g
85¢
BUILD A HOUSE FOR MARTINS

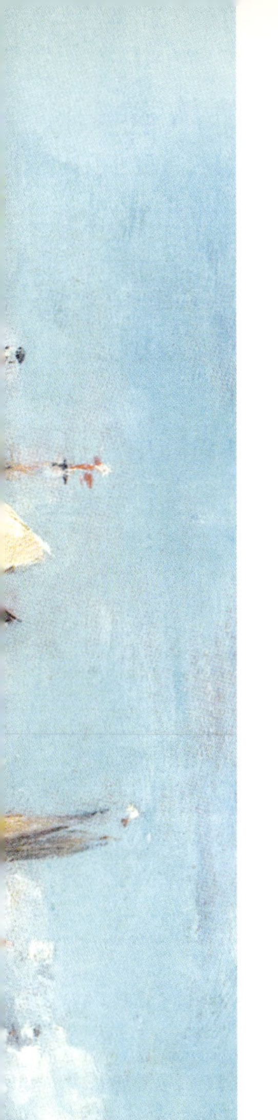
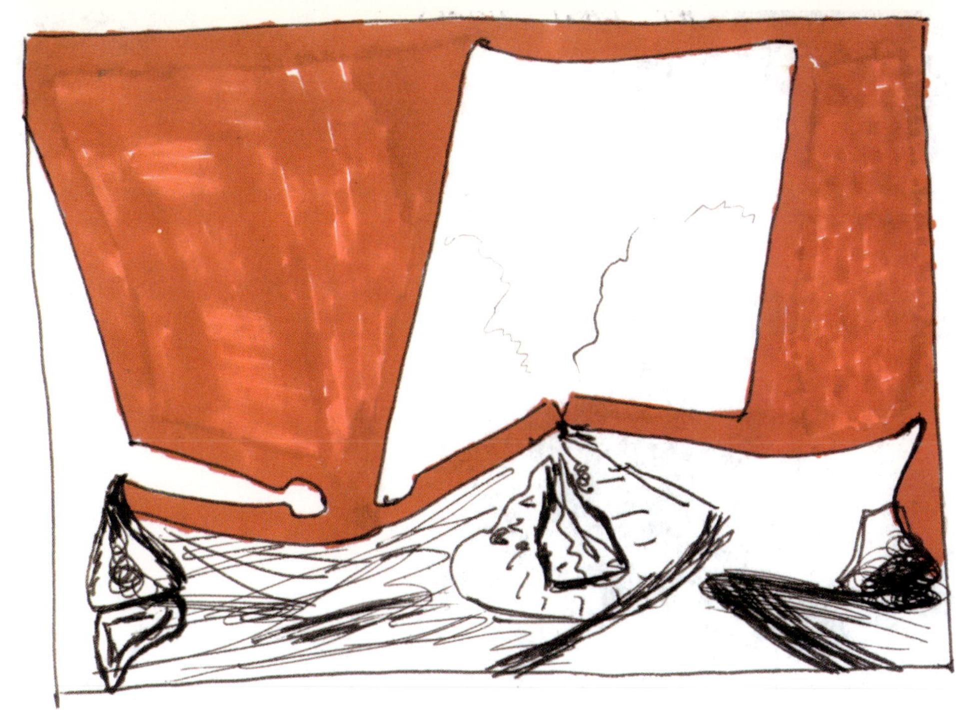
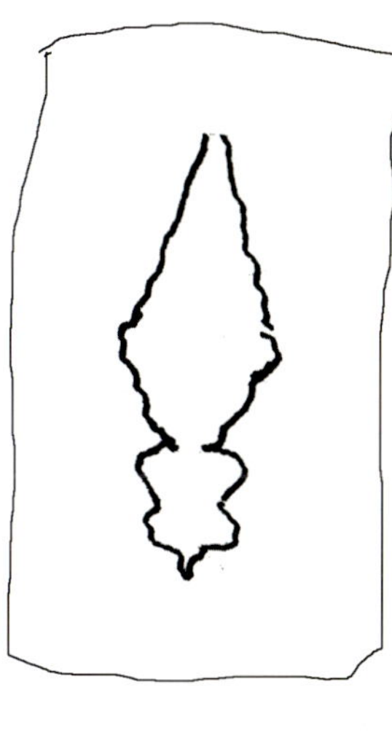
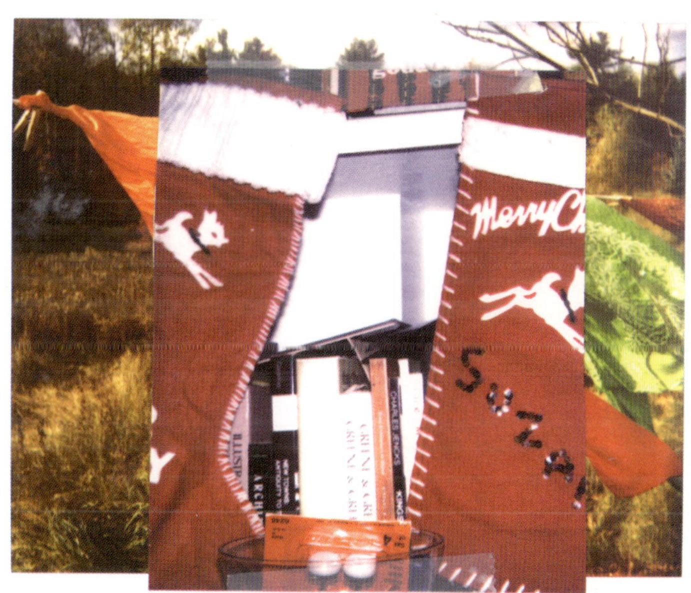
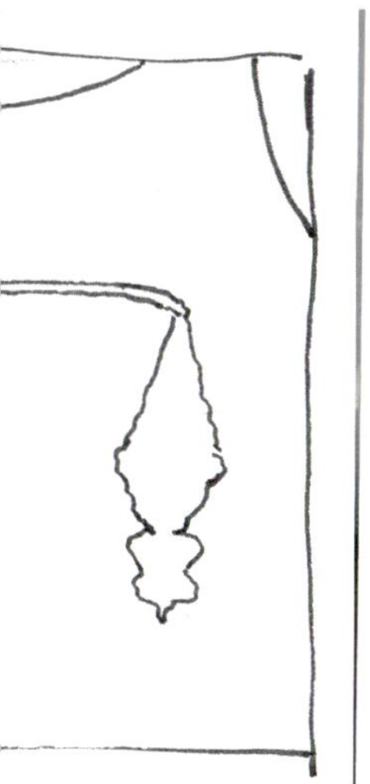
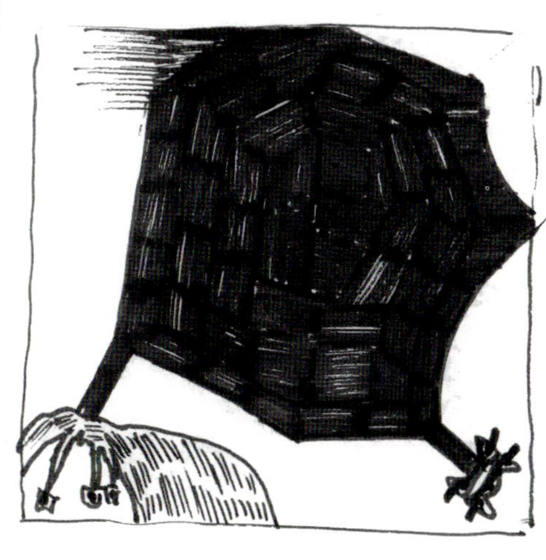
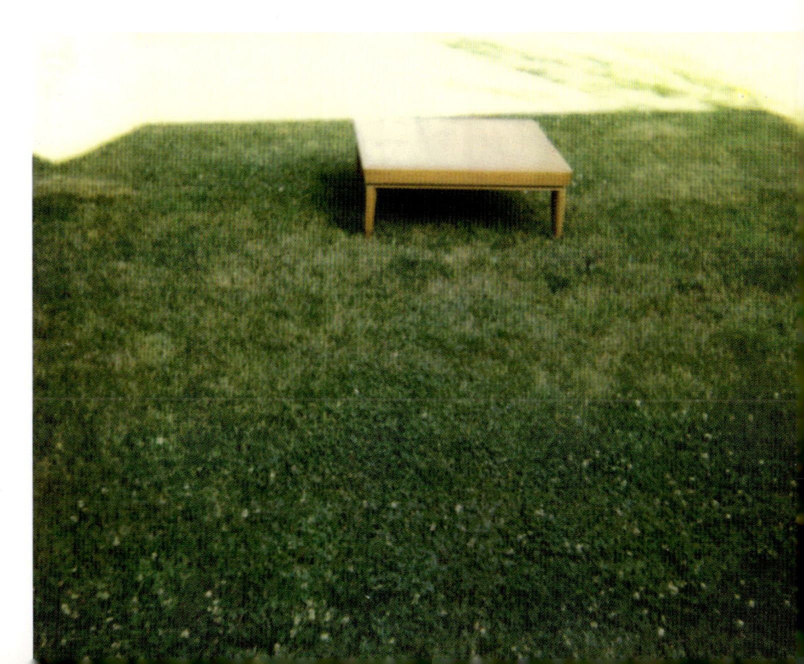

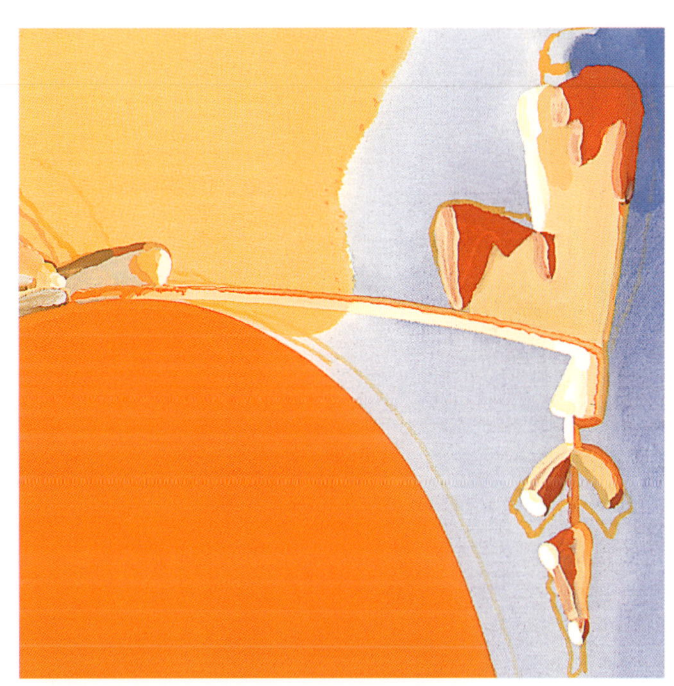

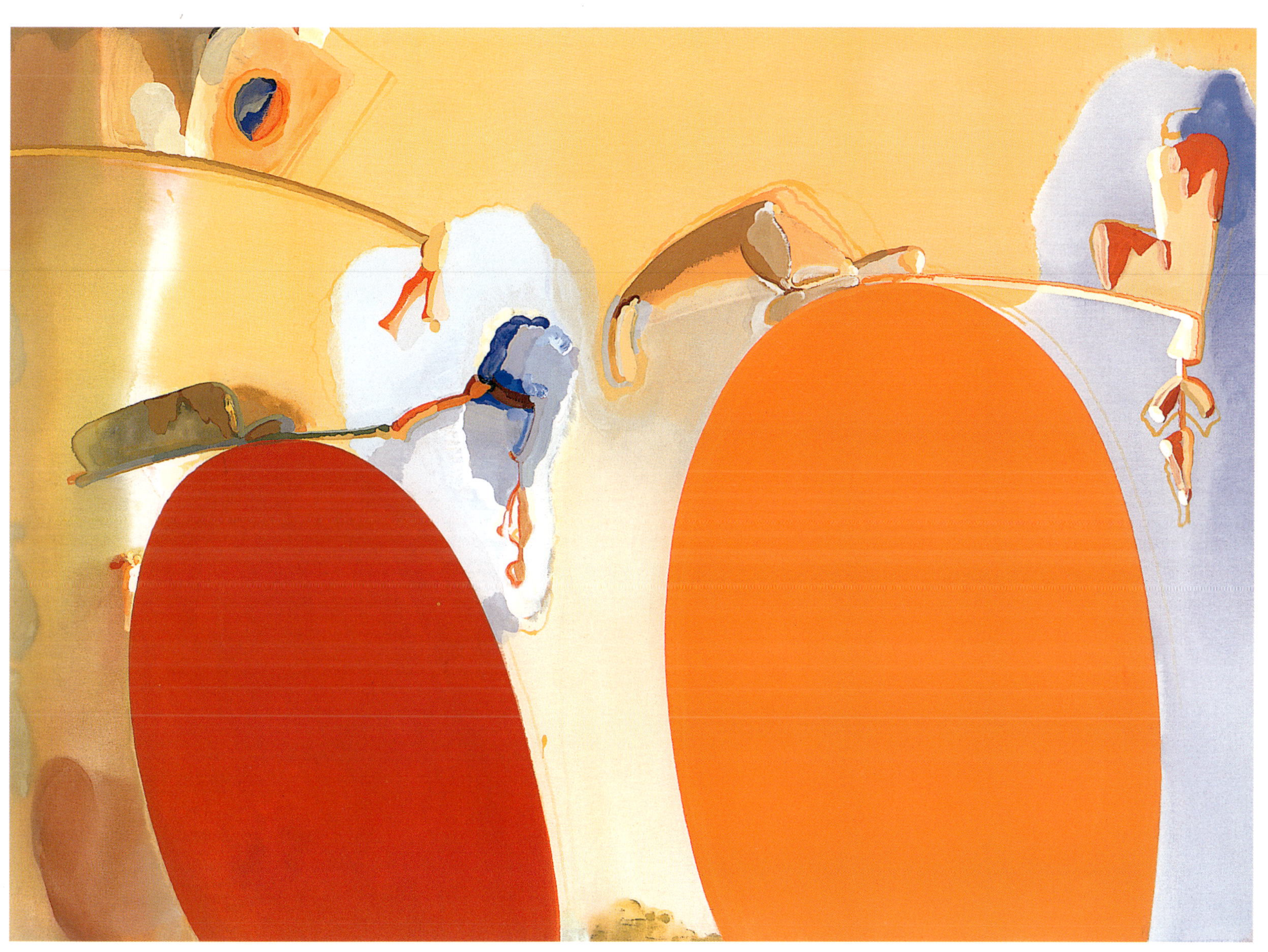

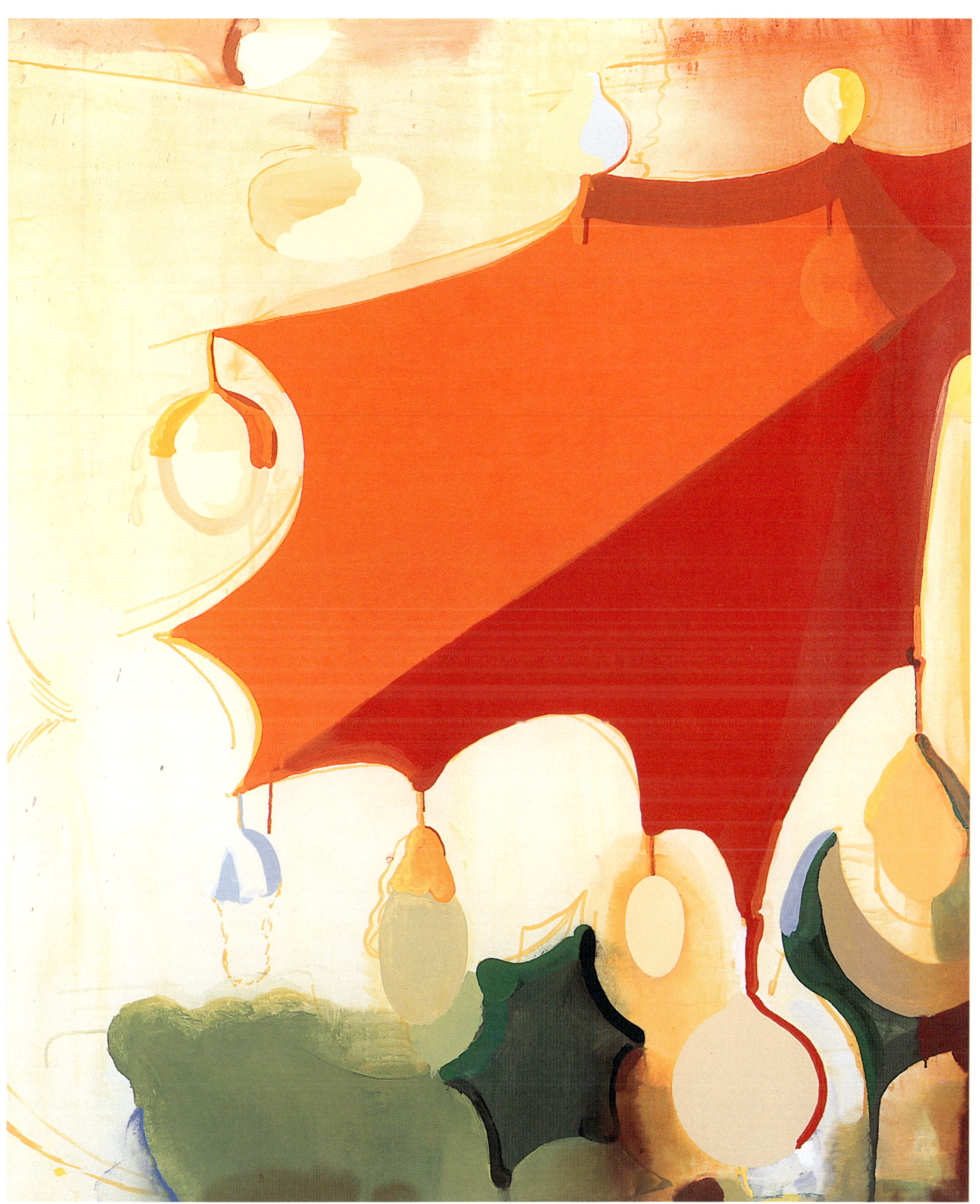

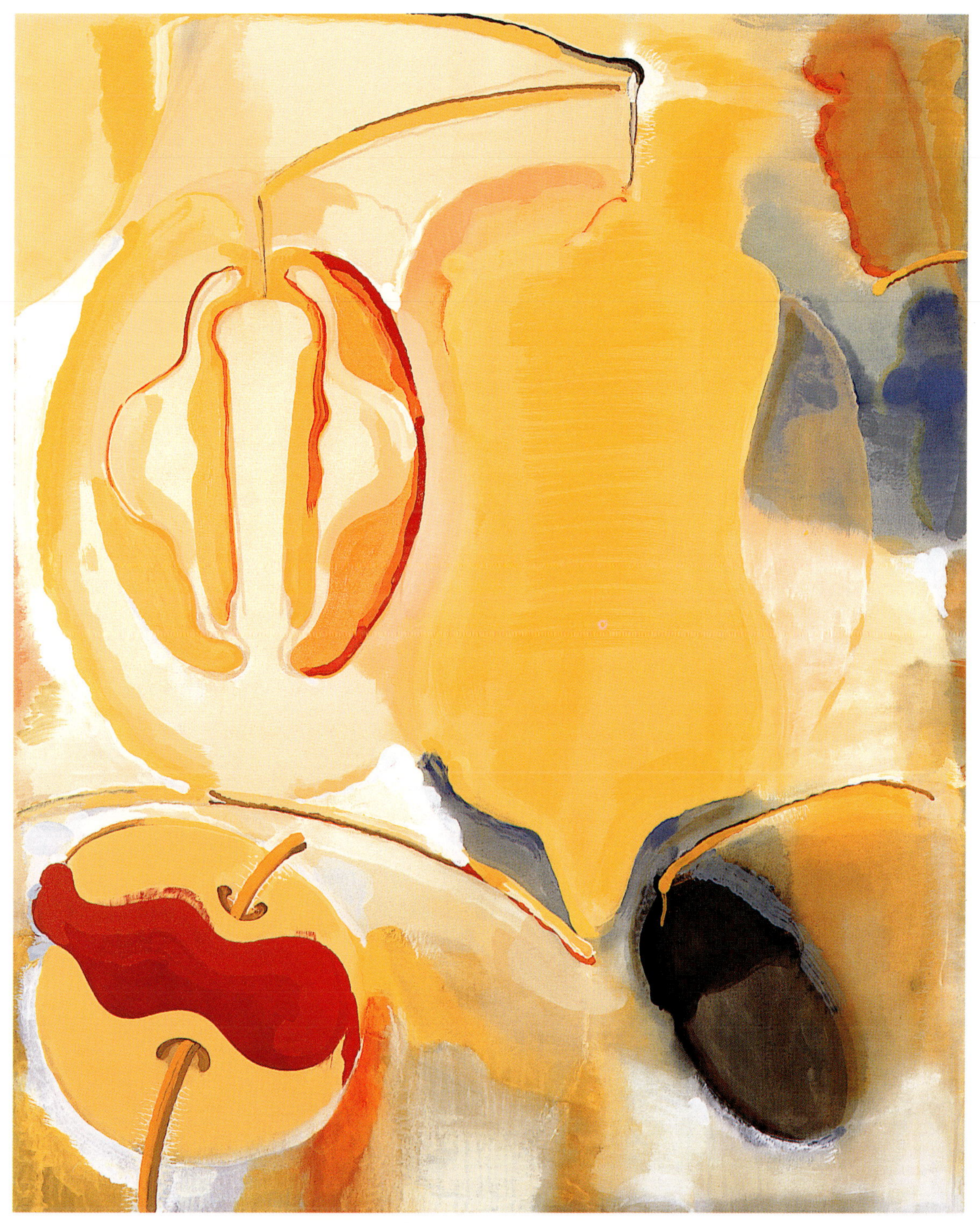

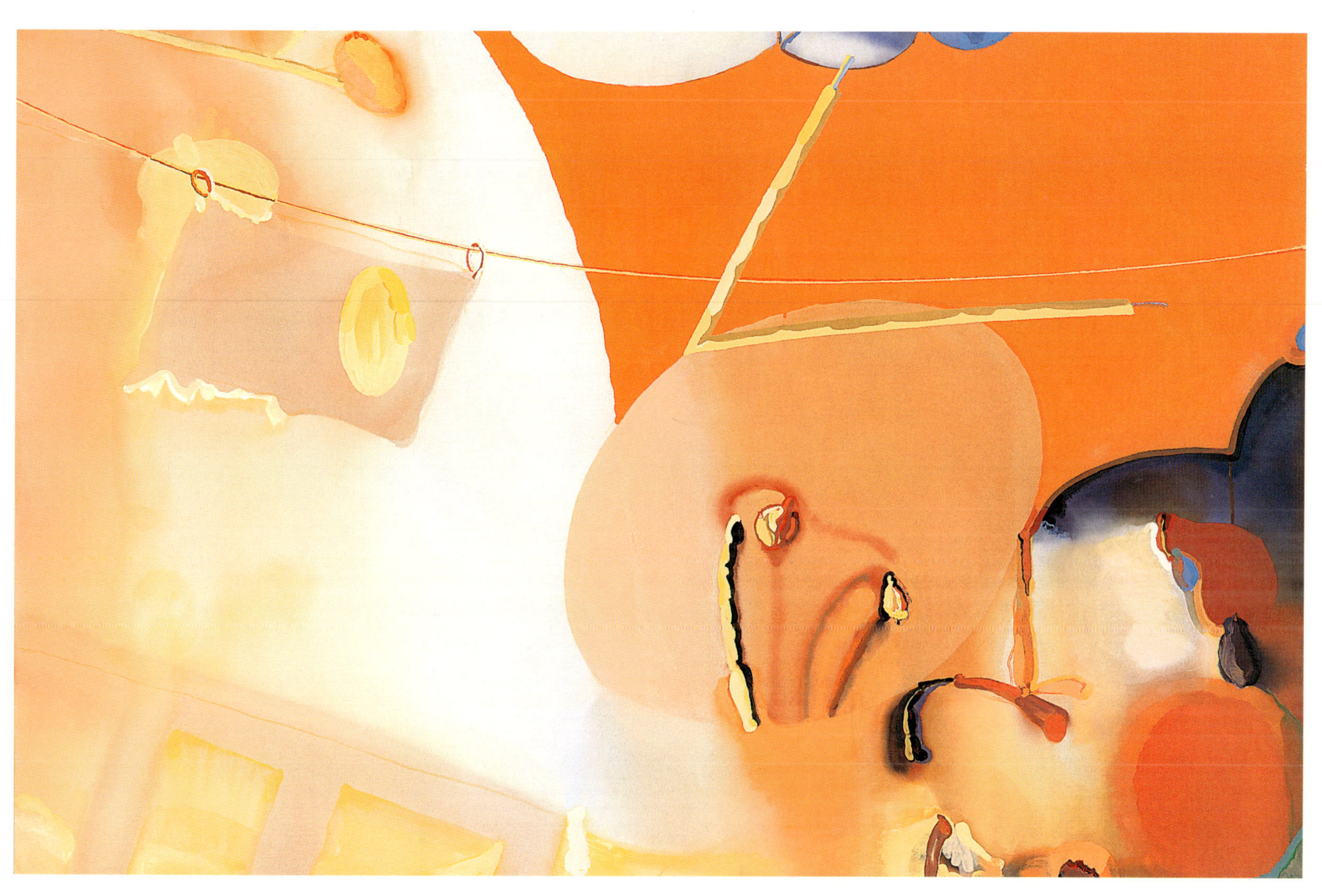

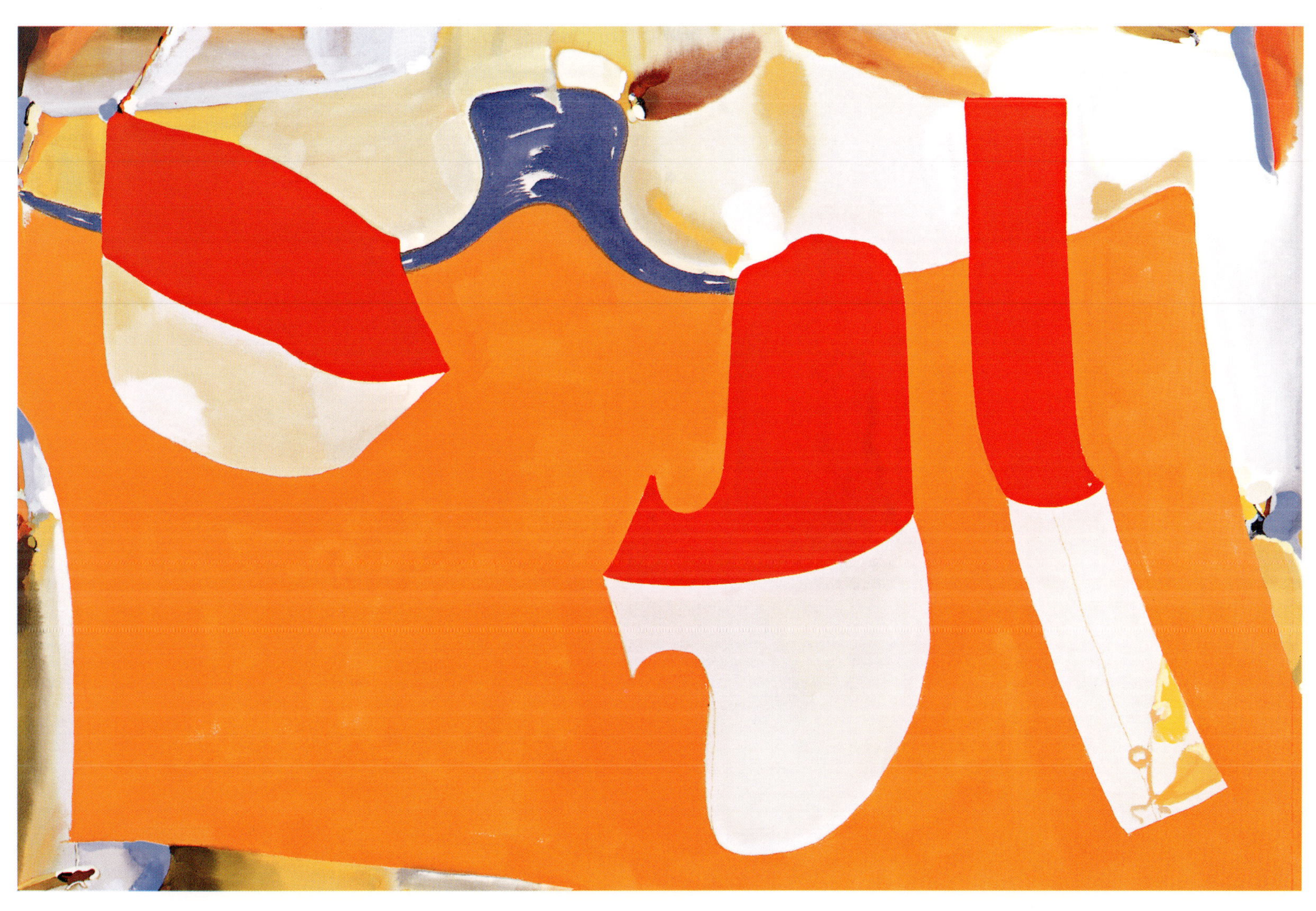

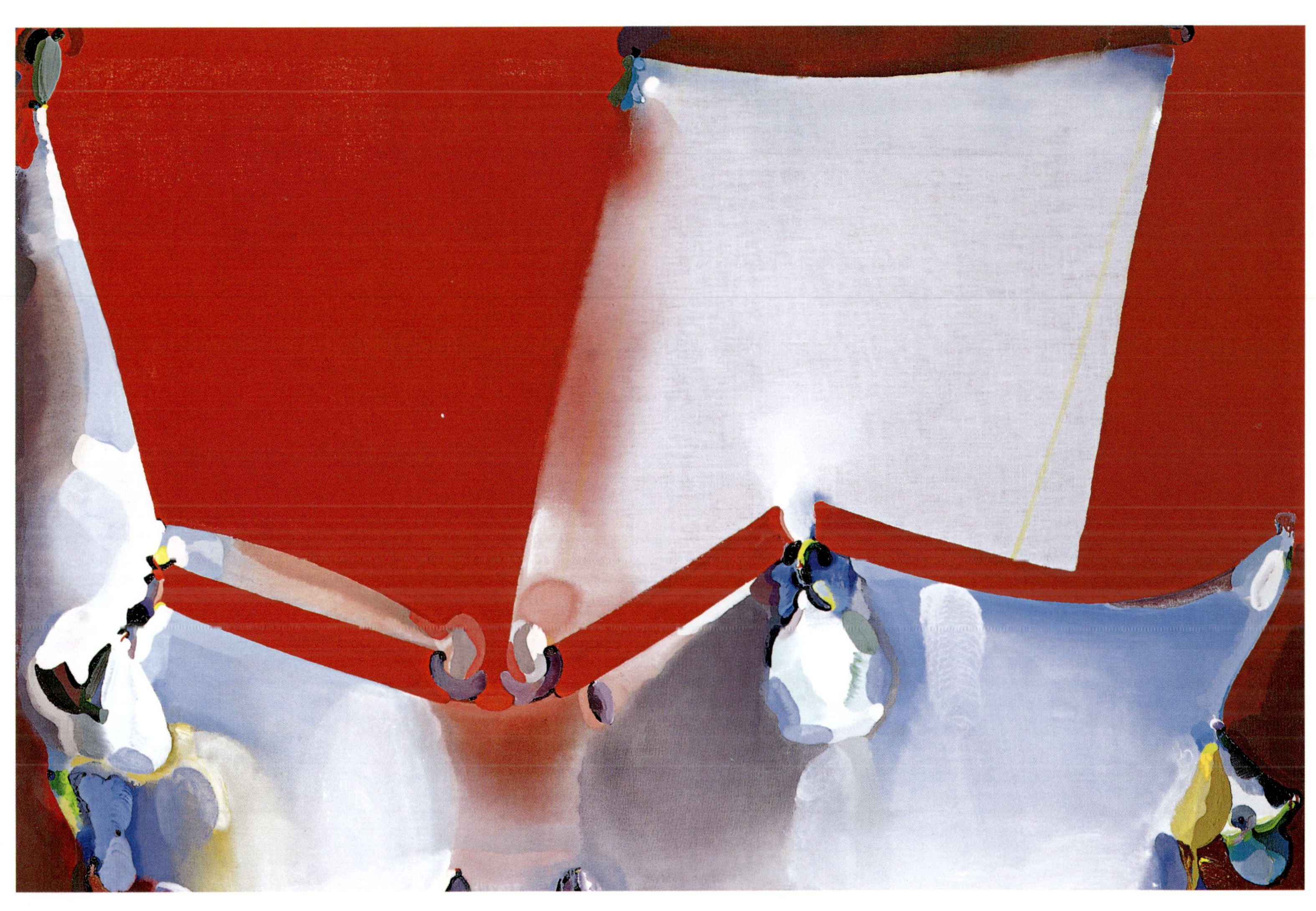

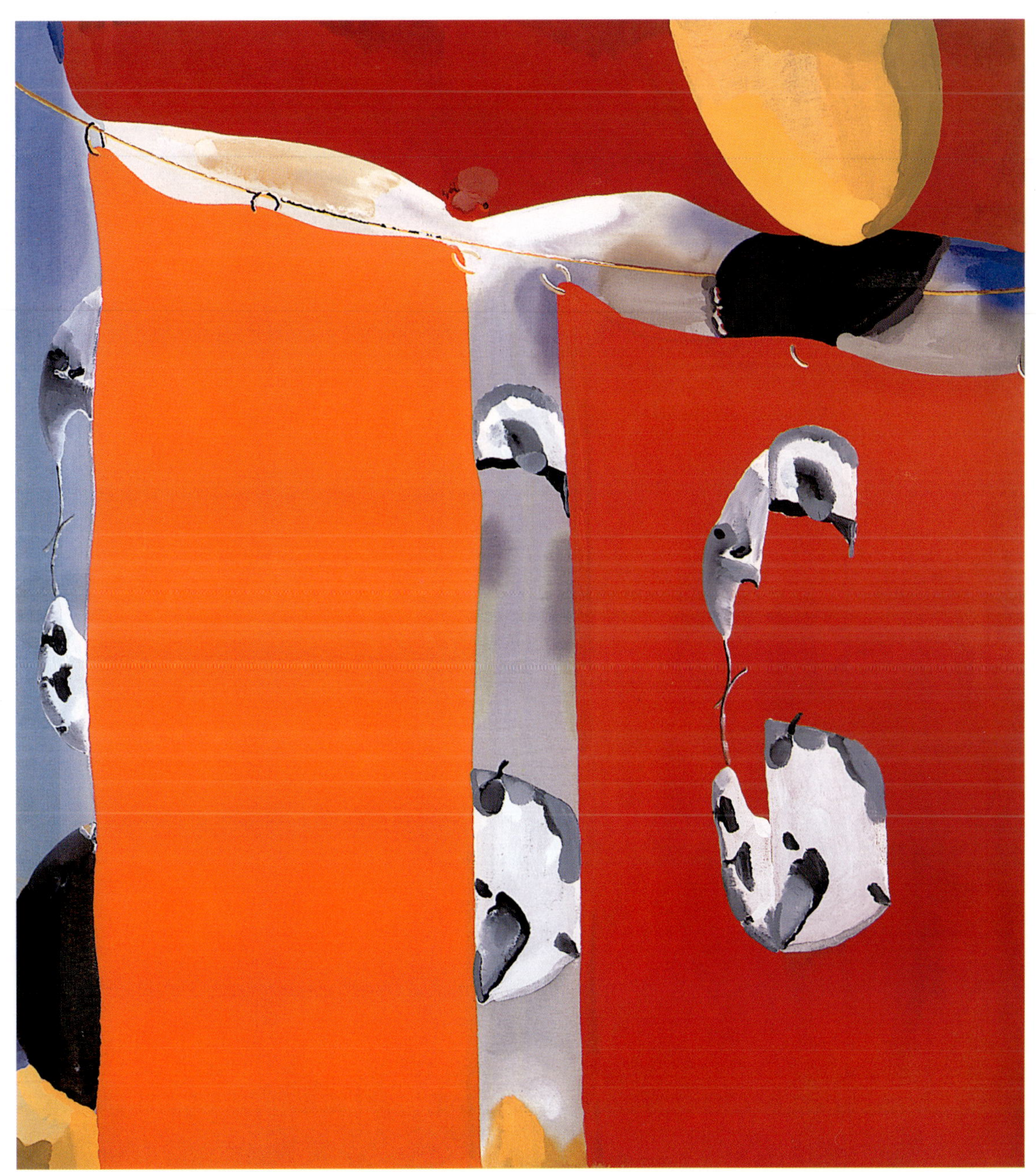

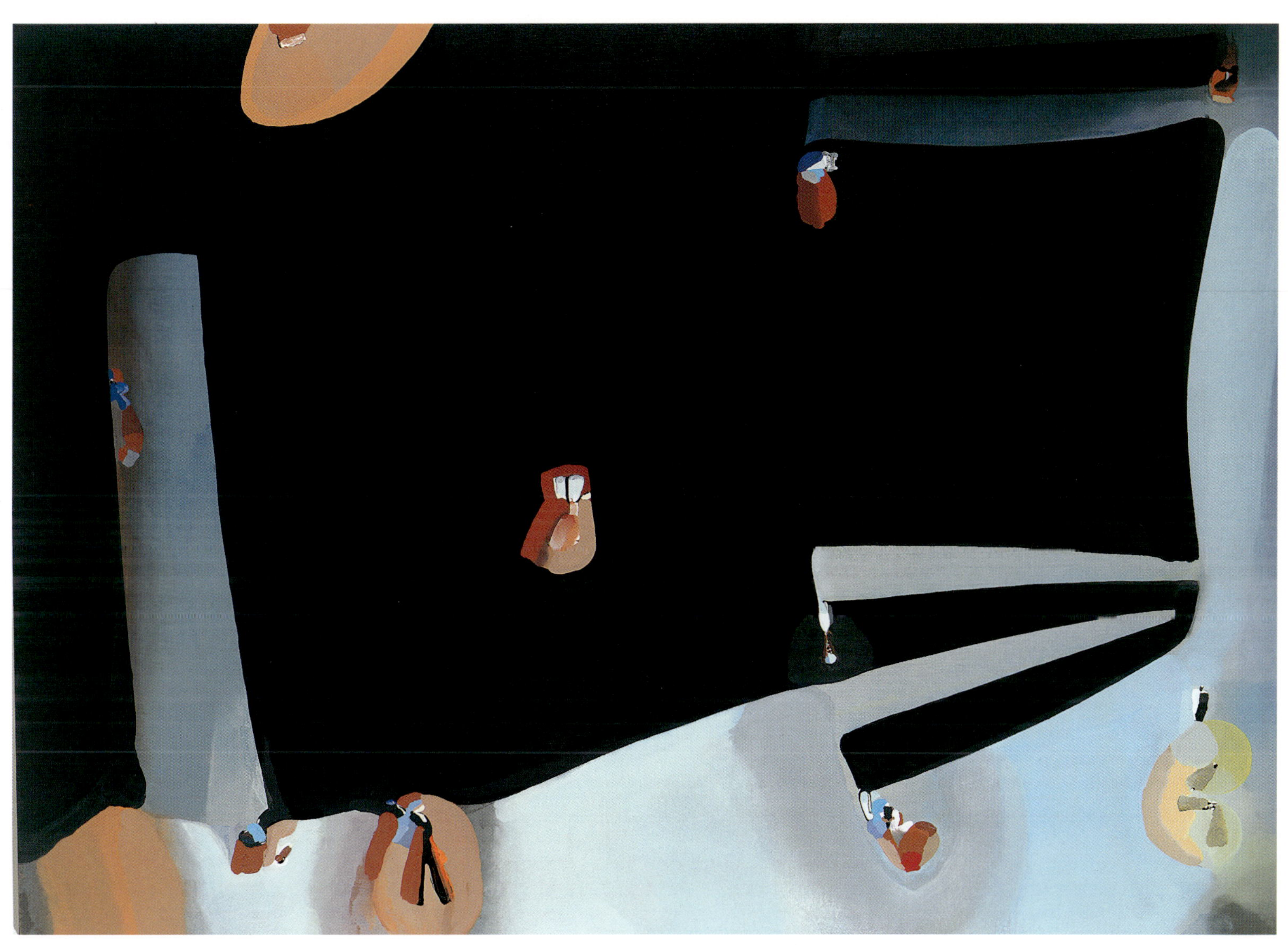

Plates